Historic Places

Samantha Bell

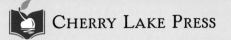

CHERRY LAKE PRESS

Published in the United States of America by Cherry Lake Publishing Group
Ann Arbor, Michigan
www.cherrylakepublishing.com

Reading Adviser: Beth Walker Gambro, MS, Ed., Reading Consultant, Yorkville, IL

Photo Credits: cover, title page: © f11photo/Shutterstock; page 4: © Joseph Creamer/Shutterstock; page 5: © Christopher Mazmanian/Shutterstock; page 7: © Christoph Schaarschmidt/Shutterstock; page 8: NPS Photo; Page 11: © Jon Bilous/Shutterstock; page 12: NPS Photo; page 13: © Ovidiu Hrubaru/Shutterstock; page 14: © Carol R Montoya/Dreamstime.com; page 17: © Lei Xu/Dreamstime.com; page 18: © Jiawangkun/Dreamstime.com; page 21: NPS Photo/ Beth Parnicza; page 22: NPS Photo/ Beth Parnicza; page 23: NPS Photo; page 24: NPS Photo; page 25: NPS Photo; page 27: NPS Photo; page 29: NPS Photo; page 30: © Elen33/Dreamstime.com

Cherry Lake Press is an imprint of Cherry Lake Publishing Group.

Library of Congress Cataloging-in-Publication Data

Names: Bell, Samantha, author.
Title: Historic places / written by Samantha Bell.
Description: Ann Arbor, Michigan : Cherry Lake Publishing, [2024] | Series: National park adventures | Audience: Grades 4-6 | Summary: "Walk in the footsteps of founders on this adventure through history. This title introduces readers to the ancient Indigenous homes of Mesa Verde and the forts, battlefields, and halls that shaped our nation today. Part of our 21st Century Skills Library, this series introduces concepts of natural sciences and social studies centered around a sense of adventure"— Provided by publisher.
Identifiers: LCCN 2023010566 | ISBN 9781668928479 (paperback) |
    ISBN 9781668929940 (ebook) | ISBN 9781668931424 (pdf)
Subjects: LCSH: Historic sites—United States—Juvenile literature. | National parks and reserves—United States—Juvenile literature. | National monuments—United States—Juvenile literature.
Classification: LCC E159 .B413 2024 | DDC 973—dc23/eng/20230407
LC record available at https://lccn.loc.gov/2023010566

Cherry Lake Publishing Group would like to acknowledge the work of the Partnership for 21st Century Learning, a Network of Battelle for Kids. Please visit http://www.battelleforkids.org/networks/p21 for more information.

Printed in the United States of America
Corporate Graphics

Note from publisher: Websites change regularly, and their future contents are outside of our control. Supervise children when conducting any recommended online searches for extended learning opportunities.

Samantha Bell was born and raised near Orlando, Florida. She grew up in a family of eight kids and all kinds of pets, including goats, chickens, cats, dogs, rabbits, horses, parakeets, hamsters, guinea pigs, a monkey, a raccoon, and a coatimundi. She now lives with her family in the foothills of the Blue Ridge Mountains, where she enjoys hiking, painting, and snuggling with their cats Pocket, Pebble, and Mr. Tree-Tree Triggers.

CONTENTS

Introduction

The National Park sites help protect the land's natural beauty and resources. They also preserve important historical places. They help visitors understand the people, places, and experiences that have shaped the country. Whether cliff dwellings, protective forts, or an underground railroad, these places present the stories of America's past.

CHAPTER 1

Cliff Dwellings

Mesa Verde National Park, Colorado

Around 550, the Ancestral Pueblo people moved to Mesa Verde in what is now southwestern Colorado. Mesa Verde is a region of deep canyons and tall landforms. Many of the landforms have wide, flat tops. They are called *mesas*, the Spanish word for "table." The Ancestral Pueblo people lived on the mesas. They built houses, villages, and farms. Some of the landforms had overhanging cliffs on the side. Around 1200, the Ancestral Pueblo people built new villages beneath the cliffs. They built homes, community centers, and kivas. The kivas were special rooms used for ceremonies or political meetings.

Cliff Palace from the Mesa Verde cliff dwellings in Mesa Verde National Park

Ladders and steps connect different levels of Cliff Palace.

The Ancestral Pueblo people created these buildings with rectangular blocks made of **sandstone**. Some buildings were roughly built, while others had well-shaped stones. Some buildings were decorated inside with painted designs. The people lived in the cliff dwellings for about 100 years. Then they began moving to the south into what is now New Mexico and Arizona. No one is sure why. A severe drought may have been the reason. Without much rain, they may not have been able to grow enough food. By 1300, the cliff dwellings were empty.

Even though the people left, the buildings they constructed still stand. Today, the park helps preserve more than 600 cliff dwellings. Some of them are one-room houses. Others are community centers with more than 100 rooms. Visitors to the park can tour five different villages. Cliff Palace is the largest. It contains 150 rooms and 23 kivas. Another village called Longhouse is about the same size. Spruce Tree House is the third-largest village. It includes about 130 rooms and eight kivas. Balcony House has 38 rooms and two kivas. Step House is the smallest village. It is the only one that visitors can tour on their own.

BETTER THAN CATTLE

In December 1888, two cowboys were riding across the mesa. Their names were Richard Wetherill and Charlie Mason. They were looking for some stray cattle. They came to a vast canyon. They saw something that looked like a city in the cliffs. They made their way to the city and began exploring. The buildings reminded them of **medieval** castles they had read about in books. They named the city Cliff Palace. Wetherill and Mason spent many years exploring the cliff dwellings. They discovered almost every cliff dwelling in Mesa Verde.

CHAPTER 2

Castillo de San Marcos

Castillo de San Marcos National Monument, Florida

The first Spanish explorer arrived in Florida in 1513. By 1565, the Spanish had established a settlement named Saint Augustine. The settlement had **fortifications** made of wood. But during the next 100 years, Saint Augustine suffered many enemy assaults. Pirates, Native Americans, and French and British forces attacked the settlement. They destroyed the fortifications. The Spanish replaced them nine times. Finally, after a pirate raid in 1668, the governor of the colony asked officials for money for a better defense system. The Spanish rulers approved plans to build a stone fortress. In 1672, construction of Castillo de San Marcos began.

A view of Castillo de San Marcos at sunset in St. Augustine, Florida

Castillo is the Spanish word for "castle." The new fortress looked like a castle. Diamond-shaped **bastions** were added to the fort walls. Each one had a circular tower. The Spanish mounted cannons on the bastions. The bastions provided protection from every side. There was only one way in or out of the fort. A drawbridge protected this entrance. In the years that followed, the Castillo withstood many attacks. Control of the fort changed between the British and Spanish until the U.S. government gained control of it in 1821. The U.S. Army used the fort until 1899.

The drawbridge at Castillo de San Marcos protected the entrance to the fort.

Visitors to Castillo de San Marcos can tour
the fort at their own pace.

With such a long history, Castillo de San Marcos is the country's oldest **masonry** fort. Visitors can explore the fort at their own pace. They can go inside rooms once used for soldiers or prisoners. They can also go out on the gun decks to view the city of St. Augustine. Some rangers and volunteers are dressed in **period-style** clothing. They share stories about the colonists who lived at the fort. Visitors can even watch cannon and musket demonstrations.

BUILDING WITH SHELLS

Wooden forts did not hold up against attacks. So when it was time to build the new fort, the Spanish tried something different. **Coquina** rocks are made from tiny coquina clam shells. The coast of Florida is one of the few places where this rock is found. The Spanish used coquina rocks to build the new fort. They knew it would not burn like the wooden forts. But they did not know how strong it would be. The first attack on the new fort came in 1702. The cannonballs did not break the stone. Instead, the cannonballs bounced off of the stone or sank into it slightly.

CHAPTER 3

Independence Hall

Independence National Historic Park, Pennsylvania

In 1732, the colony of Pennsylvania began building a place where its government could meet. Known as the State House, the building was finally finished in 1753. Twenty-two years later, the American Revolution (1775–1789) began. The 13 American colonies wanted to be free of British rule. Pennsylvania loaned the building to the Second Continental Congress, the government for the colonies. The Congress met in the Assembly Room. The next year, a five-man committee wrote the Declaration of Independence. Committee member Thomas Jefferson was the main author. Congress members signed the document in the State House. In 1787, representatives from the new states again gathered in the State House

Independence Hall's clock tower, cupola, and steeple

The Declaration of Independence and the U.S. Constitution were signed in the Assembly Room of Independence Hall.

for the Constitutional Convention. After many debates, the members wrote a new document called the Constitution. It established the powers of the government and basic laws for the country. The Constitution was signed in the State House, too.

The Declaration of Independence and the Constitution promote the principles of freedom and democracy. The State House played an important part in American history. But people soon lost interest in the building. By the early 1800s, Pennsylvania's state government had moved to another city. The building fell into disrepair. In 1824, a Revolutionary War hero and friend of

President George Washington visited from France. His name was Marquis de Lafayette. People decorated the Assembly Room of the State House for Lafayette. He called the house the "birthplace of independence."

Many years later, the building's name had become officially known as Independence Hall. Today, it is called the "birthplace of America." Visitors can take a tour led by a park ranger. The visitors stand in the same room where the Declaration of Independence and the Constitution were signed. Also in the room is the Rising Sun Chair. This chair is engraved with an image of a rising sun. George Washington sat in this chair during the Constitutional Convention.

A SYMBOL FOR FREEDOM

In 1751, a member of the Pennsylvania Assembly ordered a metal bell for the State House. It cracked the first time it was rung. Local metalworkers melted down the bell and made a new one. Its tone was not very good, so they recast it again. The bell rang to call people together on special occasions. It also called lawmakers to their meetings. The bell's **inscription** says, "Proclaim liberty throughout all the land unto all the inhabitants thereof." Known as the Liberty Bell, it later became a symbol of freedom from slavery. It eventually cracked and was moved to a display near Independence Hall.

CHAPTER 4

Harriet Tubman Underground Railroad National Historic Park

Dorchester County, Maryland

Harriet Tubman was born into slavery around 1822. She spent her childhood working on farms in Dorchester County, Maryland. When Harriet was just 5 years old, her owner hired her out to other households. When she was 12, she went to work in the fields. One day, Harriet saw an enslaved man in a grocery store. He did not have permission to be there. He tried to run from the overseer, who was

Flat wetlands near the visitor center of Harriet Tubman Underground Railroad National Historic Park Visitor Center

Sunrise over the visitor center in Harriet Tubman Underground Railroad National Historic Park

in charge of the enslaved people. Harriet helped him by blocking the overseer's way. The overseer picked up a heavy metal weight and threw it at the enslaved man. But he hit Harriet in the head instead. She never completely recovered.

In 1849, it seemed as if Harriet and the other enslaved people would be sold. She ran away and escaped to Pennsylvania. There, Harriet worked as a paid household servant and saved her money. She wanted to help other enslaved people escape. Harriet spent the next 10 years rescuing enslaved people in Maryland. These included her parents, brothers, and friends. She became part of the Underground Railroad. This group of people helped lead enslaved African Americans to freedom in Canada. In all, Harriet led about 70 enslaved people to freedom.

MUCH TO REMEMBER

Two national park sites are dedicated to Harriet Tubman. The park in Dorchester County remembers her early life and her role with the Underground Railroad. The second site is the Harriet Tubman National Historical Park in Auburn, New York. This site tells the story of her life after the Civil War. It includes the house she owned. It includes buildings she donated to become a home for the elderly. The site also includes the church that she raised money to build. Across the street from this park is Fort Hill Cemetery. People can visit Harriet Tubman's grave there.

Visitors listen to a tour guide speak about the Bucktown Store, where Harriet Tubman sustained her head injury.

Stewart's Canal is located within Harriet Tubman Underground Railroad National Historic Park.

The Harriet Tubman Underground Railroad National Historic Park was created to remember Harriet's childhood. It is located at the site of the plantation where Harriet was enslaved as a girl. It also includes the site of the store where she suffered her head injury. Visitors to the park can see where Harriet grew up. The landscapes in the area still look much like they did when Harriet lived there. The park also includes the home site of a free Black man named Jacob Jackson. He helped Harriet in her efforts to free other enslaved people. The visitor center includes exhibits and a theater that tells about Harriet Tubman's life and work.

CHAPTER 5

Fort Sumter National Monument

Fort Sumter and Fort Moultrie National Historical Park, South Carolina

Fort Sumter is a five-sided fort located in Charleston Harbor in South Carolina. It was named for General Thomas Sumter, a Revolutionary War hero. After the War of 1812 (1812–1815) with Great Britain, U.S. leaders realized the country needed better defenses along the coasts. They planned to build about 200 new forts, including Fort Sumter. Construction began in 1829. The fort was going to house 650 men and 135 cannons. But the fort was never finished. Only 15 cannons were brought there. U.S. soldiers occupied the fort anyway.

An aerial view of Fort Sumter in Charleston Harbor

ONE LIFE LOST

No one was killed when the Confederates fired on Fort Sumter. But one person was accidentally killed after the Union troops surrendered. Before they left, the troops lowered the U.S. flag flying over the fort. They honored it with a 100-gun salute. The 100 cannons were fired one at a time. But as they were shooting, one of the cannons fired early. It caused an explosion that injured three men and killed Private Daniel Hough of the 1st U.S. Artillery. His was the first death of the Civil War.

In December 1860, South Carolina **seceded** from the United States. It joined six other states to become the Confederate States of America. The remaining states were known as the Union. Confederate leaders wanted the Union troops to leave the fort. But the U.S. government planned to send the troops more supplies. On April 11, 1861, three Confederate officials met with the fort's commander, Major Robert Anderson. They promised Anderson and his men safe passage out of the fort. Anderson refused to leave. The next day, Confederate forces fired on Fort Sumter. The soldiers in the fort were low on food and firepower. Less than two days later, they surrendered. The battle marked the beginning of the Civil War (1861–1865).

Visitors must ride a ferry boat to Fort Sumter.

Fort Sumter is on a human-made island built from thousands of tons of **granite**. To visit the fort, people must travel on a ferry, a small boat used for short distances. Park rangers present programs inside the fort. They answer questions about its history. Visitors on the first ferry of the day can help the rangers raise the U.S. flag over the fort. Visitors on the last ferry to leave can help them lower and fold the flag.

Activity

Plan Your Adventure!

What historic sites would you like to see? The National Park Service helps preserve historic places from coast to coast. Each site tells another part of the story of the United States. You can make a list of the sites you would like to visit. Then look through the other books in this series for more places to explore.

Sweet Structures

Many historic places in the National Park Service are houses, forts, or other buildings. You can create your own special structure. All you need is some sugar and glue.

Supplies:

Sugar cubes

Crafting glue

Before you begin, decide what kind of structure you want to make. It could be a replica of a building mentioned in this book. You could create a building like the cliff dwellings. You might make a fortress-like Castillo de San Marcos or Fort Sumter. Or you could choose to make a structure of your own design.

Next, start building! Stack the sugar cubes to make the walls of your structure. Use crafting glue to hold them together. To make a completely edible building, use icing instead of glue.

Learn More

Books

Huddleston, Emma. *Exploring Independence Hall.* Lake Elmo, MN: Focus Readers, 2020.

Mattern, Joanne. *Fort Sumter.* Vero Beach, FL: Rourke Educational Media, 2014.

McDonough, Yona Zeldis. *Who Was Harriet Tubman?* New York, NY: Penguin Workshop, 2019.

Sipperley, Keli. *Old Fort at St. Augustine.* Vero Beach, FL: Rourke Educational Media, 2014.

On the Web

With an adult, learn more online with these suggested searches.

"Castillo Virtual Tour." National Park Service.

"Independence." National Historical Park, Pennsylvania.

"Much More than Brick and Mortar: The Story of Fort Sumter National Monument." National Park Service.

"Tubman Talks: A Journey Revisited." National Park Service.

Glossary

bastions (BAS-chuhnz) parts of a fortification that extend beyond the wall at an angle

coquina (koh-KEE-nuh) a soft limestone formed of broken shells cemented together

fortifications (for-tuh-fuh-KAY-shuhnz) walls or other reinforcements built to strengthen a place against attack

granite (GRAH-nuht) a hard stone used for making buildings, monuments, and sculptures

inscription (in-SKRIP-shuhn) a short message written on a monument or other object

masonry (MAY-suhn-ree) something built with stone, brick, or cement

medieval (mee-DEE-vuhl) having to do with the Middle Ages

period-style (PIHR-ee-uhd STY-uhl) something specific to a certain era in history

sandstone (SAND-stohn) a rock formed mostly of sand and held together with a substance such as cement

seceded (sih-SEED-id) withdrew from a country or group

Index

21st
Century
Skills Library

Explore some of the most amazing places in the United States. From the highest heights to the deepest caverns and caves, take a cross-country trip to find the places that connect us all. Start your adventure now!

Read all the books in this series!

Exploring the National Parks

Amazing Heights

The Depths Below

Rarest Places

Historic Places

Monuments to Remember

Nature's Monuments

Park Life from Dinosaurs to Prairie Dogs

GRL: U

ISBN-13: 978-1668928479

9 781668 928479

CHERRYLAKEPRESS.COM

CHERRY LAKE PRESS

National Park
Adventures

The Depths Below

Samantha Bell